Green Dialogue

poems

Irene Willis

GREEN DIALOGUE

POEMS

IRENE WILLIS

International Psychoanalytic Books (IPBooks)
New York • www.IPBooks.net

Copyright 2020 by Irene Willis

International Psychoanalytic Books (IPBooks)
Queens, NY

Online at: IPBooks.net

All rights reserved. This book may not be reproduced, transmitted, or stored, in whole or in part by any means, including graphic, electronic, or mechanical without the express permission of the author and/or publisher, except in the case of brief quotations embodied in critical articles and reviews.

ISBN: 978-1-949093-74-2

for my daughter Gina
and the memory of my husband, Bernard Daves Rossell (d.2016)

Contents

I

Maxine Gone	3
My Story and Yours	5
My Brother and I	6
Sorry to Be So Long	7
Re-reading the Poets	8
At the Café	9
Depression Baby	10
The Visit	11
I Was the Girl Who Always Spoke	13
At Puberty	14
Fourteen	15
Can He Dance?	16
What They Taught	17
When Nana Had the Stroke	18
Epiphany in a Country Church	19
Roach	20
A Woman Is Her Mother	21
Mixed Feelings	23
Selling the House	24
House	25
Fresh Start	27
The Highway	28

Lonely   29
We   30
The Letters in My Dream   31
Responsible   32
Valentine   33
Ghost   34
The Urge to Kiss Animals   35
The Milking   37
Relatives   38
The Slowest Step   39
Split-Screen   41
Gratitude   42
Her Wit and Wisdom After My Divorce   43
Eve, After Banishment   44

II

New York in the 70's   48
Bully Pulpit, 2001   49
Accounting   51
Elephant   52
Crotch-grab   53
The New Man   55
Abram Returns from Battle without Spoils   56

Politics	57
To Market, To Market: An American Ghazal	58
Impeached	59
Defiant Subject	60
On Reading Howard Zinn	62
Downloadable Gun Clears Some Legal Obstacles	63
Neuticles	65
Discovery	66
Freckled Hands	67
Allergy	68
Remembering Her Life	69
Solo	70
In Grief	71
Dialogue in Green	72
Aubade for the Almost-Old	75
Old in a Time of Pandemic	76
Lockdown Sonnet	77
Fully Engaged	78
My Pleasure	79
A Life	80
Laughing Kookaburras	82
About the Author	84
Acknowledgments	86

I

Maxine Gone

In memoriam, Maxine Kumin
1925–2014

How did we end it? Was I just a fan—
or truly a friend? I thought the latter

but did it matter if the tone was right:
not lofty, hierarchical, no slight ever

only gracious, warm response
to my gentle inquiries as to health,

animals, families, mutual friends,
and always immediate? She said once

that she saved all her e-mails
in a long cardboard box just like

the ones my father's shirts came in—
perhaps her father's too, or husband's

and it felt so familiar, even cozy,
I decided *friendship* was the word

whether she would acknowledge it or not.
Did any of our exchange, I wonder

Go to Bienecke's archive with the rest
or did they stay in that long shirt box

above her desktop computer
like the basket where I store mine?

Which would be better?
I hope, somehow, the latter.

My Story and Yours

*He doesn't know the personal narrative
is obsolete.*
        —Marie Howe

Neither do I. Or I don't want to.
I love narrative. I love the personal.

And so do you, don't you—
need to hear in my story

what you know is true in yours?

I slice the fat loaf of my childhood loss,
offer it with the wine of compassion.

You forgive your father everything.

My Brother and I

Two wives, whose names began with *Ma*.
Two husbands, whose names began with *Da*.
Stuttering still, I try to say
What we longed for.

Sorry to Be So Long

–for Jim Haba

I had to wait until
I could read your poems
quietly
without the noise of every day
drumming in my ears.

Thank you for this silence.

Re-reading the Poets

So many have been hurt
into poetry
pained into poetry—
that jolt
when you read their words.

At the Café

If poetry is a café
Then poets
Are an ethnic group
That come to sip latté
And chatter
In their mother tongue.
Every so often
One of them
Gets up to dance.

Depression Baby

To open a new tube of toothpaste
after squeezing the old one
and rolling it tight.
To re-use a paper bag—long before
plastic started choking whales
and turtles.
To never spay our dogs and cats
because we didn't know about that
or even ticks.
We knew about mosquitoes, though,
and kept picking at the scabs.
Did we know about contagion at all?
Maybe not, because we got
every childhood disease
and (some of us) adult ones
we were too young to understand.
So the world was a mystery
but we celebrated
small triumphs
I remember as I throw away
another rolled-up, squeezed out
toothpaste tube.

The Visit

Scarlet fever was delirium and pain,
mostly in my ears, legs and throat—

but the nightlight in my room was nothing new;
I always had it to keep the wolves away

That hid, when I was four, in my bedroom closet.
"The Boy Who Cried Wolf" was the story my father told

When I called and called again for a drink of water
long before the fever came, because

I wanted a few minutes more before
the prayer I had to say that scared me so—

the one about taking my soul before I woke.
But now it was Christmas Eve and I was still there,

waiting to hear the sleighbells on the roof,
my brown lisle stocking hung by the radiator.

When the door creaked open, I slid down,
hiding most of my face so I could see

whoever was coming in to do something to me.
If it was a burglar or pirate, he could have all my things,

I decided, before I saw the two of them,
my parents, tiptoeing in and over

to where my empty stocking was
and *putting something in before the sleighbells came,*

then going out again and coming back
with a little tree, which they set up on my dresser

and strung with lights and paper chains,
piled gifts around, smiled, and tiptoed out.

Incinerate was what they told me later
would have to happen to my toys,

my books, pajamas, bathrobe, quilt—
and it meant *burn,* and everything I loved

would then go up in smoke, would turn to ash—
and so it did, but I, whose soul was still glued tight,

saw daylight filter through my window blind.

I Was the Girl Who Always Spoke

–for Maria Mazziotti Gillan

Jolley was my name
till marriage pushed me
to the end of the alphabet.
But in second grade
a teacher told me it *wasn't*.
When she first called our names
she read mine as Joly (long o),
so I raised my hand
as I had been taught to do
and—taking a breath—
corrected her—*corrected
a teacher.*
"It's Jolley," I said.
"No, it's NOT!" she shouted.
"Jolly means to be happy.
Your name is Joly! (again with the long o).
I gasped, face hot. Kids who knew me gaped.
Lunchtime, I ran home crying.
I knew my name. I know I knew my name.
And to the end of my days
I will not forget yours, Miss Holweg.

At Puberty

My mother turned her back on me.
Was it the bleeding and the breasts?

Was it my fresh mouth—

or all of that?

I couldn't help my growing-up,
all but the hurrying—

and how

I needed to get out.

Fourteen

Fourteen was crazy.
Fourteen was weird.
Fourteen was getting home
and in my bed before
my mother found out
what I had been up to.
What *had* I been up to?
I'm peeking out
from under the covers now
and I don't even want
to tell *you*.

Can He Dance?

My parents were wonderful dancers—
only not with each other. With
each other was before I was born,
I guess, from my mother's stories
of how she judged a man.
As if I didn't know what that
was a stand-in for.

"Is he a good dancer?" my delicate
mother would ask—a question which,
because I knew the subtext,
clammed me up. We knew too much,
we kids. Do young girls giggle
over the size of a man's proboscis still?
It's so long since I knew.

What They Taught

A lot was about eating:
don't butter a whole slice
then fold it in half
and stick it in your mouth.

Some was about faces:
don't make them
keep yours straight
no staring
or grimacing

Some about stance:
hands off your hips
don't swing your arms
head up
when you walk

Bedtime was a mystery:
hands outside the covers
But *why?*
I didn't want cold shoulders
even then.

When Nana Had the Stroke

Aunt Florence said don't come;
It's better if you don't,
so I didn't.

My mother said don't go;
you'll be sorry of you do,
so I didn't.

These women who knew everything
gave orders I obeyed
and then they went.

Now that they're gone
I want to call them back
to comb my Aunt Flo's long white hair

and coax the stories out of her,
the ones she was afraid to tell
and I was afraid to hear.

Epiphany in a Country Church

I'd heard of spiritual awakenings
but—really—this was mine.
In a church, of all places,
long after childhood,
listening to, of all things, a *sermon*.
Yes, *me*. A church!
A *sermon!* Delivered with a N.Y. accent.
Heavy. Hell's Kitchen. Later
I found out I was right. He had been
a New York City cop, got religion and
now was here, preaching in a little
country church in Bucks County, PA.,
which is where I had my epiphany.
He was talking about the Sabbath,
the meaning of the word. Its root.
Which I, for all my interest in words,
had never known. Every seventh
day, he said, we need a rest. Like God.
Oh boy! I thought. *Do* I!
When I got back to work, I applied
for a sabbatical. And, by God, I got it.

Roach

Because I saw a roach
I figured there must be more
so I took my mother out
of the apartment she loved
and bought a big house
we could barely afford
with a downstairs bedroom
and bathroom for her
stuck her in it, feeling virtuous
and then, good daughter that I was
went off to work, sentencing her
to new bouts of loneliness and
despair so great she begged—yes
to go (horror of horrors) to a
nursing home.
What sins don't we commit
when sure we know what's best?
Did I say *we?* I mean *I*—
this time not the least bit grandiose.
Not even self-affirming, as I beg
her loving (?) spirit for forgiveness.

A Woman Is Her Mother

"That's the main thing,"
Anne Sexton said
some time before
she killed herself.
When I heard the news
I was in my car, parked
in my White Plains garage,
having just come home
from a workshop in N.Y.
where I was trying
to become like her.
Heartbroken about
someone I had never met
except from my seat
at the 92nd Street Y
I took myself upstairs
opened the door
and sat down again
at—yes—my Royal
portable, with a blank
sheet of paper.
Still *me*. Single then,
very much divorced
and with all that
empty paper.
Anne would be
about my age now, as I am
my mother's
Am *I* my mother?

The line was in a poem
called "Housewife"
which I never wanted to be.
So I'm not, and here
I sit, having just filled
my computer printer
with a stack from
a fresh new ream.

Mixed Feelings

*Great art is clear thinking
about mixed feelings.*
       –John Baldarassi

I can't guarantee this is clear,
Dear Reader, but simply ask:
Whoever had a feeling that *wasn't*?
Aren't all feelings somewhat mixed?
Isn't that what Freud taught us
about ourselves?
What, after all, is ambivalence?
Why do so many feel the need
to ask Ann Landers
or Dear Abby?
Consult their horoscopes?
I'm neither ambidextrous
nor pure of heart
yet might have felt
unmixed joy
but surely not love
for isn't love itself
an alloy?

Selling the House

How can we let this happen
another time?

We're leaving this house.
We're selling this house.

And these words
will disappear from the page

before the ink dries.

House

Back at the house that used to be
my house

there will be a closed dog door
Invisible Fence still in the ground

fighting the grass once more
for status

my flowers—rhododendrons
already in bloom

soon upright lilacs, big-headed dahlias
drooping over the fence

and neighbors calling the man
to open the pool.

I would be saying hello to all
on my walk

The postman would be at our box
with lots of mail

and my husband, still in his chair,
phone at his side

so he could lead me home
from where I am now

in the middle of nowhere
everywhere.

Fresh Start

Her son calls—
wondering about the meaning of life
and whether his is worth anything
now that he is thirty-five
the age when she began
questioning it all, too.
In her kitchen she remembers
how she found her own answer:
changing homes—a revival
of spirit, the great sweep of change
behind the refrigerator
a miracle that never happened
unless they were about to move,
emptying boxes a pleasure equal
to that of filling them,
the newness of dishes stacked
on shelves in a different direction,
books where they weren't before,
carpets back from the cleaner's
in rolls tied with cord, the joy
of unwrapping, crackling tissue,
smell of cleaning fluid, bleach
like salts held under the nose.

The Highway

Back when I still had
a flip-phone
and my husband
(*oh, my husband*)
disdained even that

he once had to hike
from the highway
through the woods
to a closed country club
and then to a roadside

phone booth
to call me
to rescue him
when his ancient Volvo
finally gave up.

With hardly any landmark
but his need
(*oh, his need*)
I found him
in the middle of nothing.

Lonely

Does loneliness afflict us all?
she wondered.

Is it truly deadly, as they say?
What then to do?

She let the louver close
and turned her back.

The light was blinding anyway.
Who needed it?

Opening the door, she saw
the morning paper—

bold headline now
a momentary gift.

No, more than that:
she'd spend the morning with it

and, mercifully,
the light was bright enough.

We

I envy those
who can still say *we*
in that casual way:
we did this, *we* did that.

What comes out of me now
is most often, *I*—
to the point
that I'm always

talking about myself
which of course I am
since there is no *we*
of me any more.

So why doesn't *we*
Seem self-centered, too?
I know what *I* think. You?
If you're part of a *we*,

don't answer.

The Letters in My Dream

Waking, I realized
I had been writing to my father,
telling him all that had happened
in the forty years since he died—
all in *my* life, that is, not the world's
because I figured he already knew
about that. Smart man, he'd be
120 now—so he must be really dead
despite my misgivings at the morgue
that I'd buried a stranger—one without
the scar on his chin I wouldn't let them
shave his beard to find.
If he were still alive
I would have heard from him, I know.
His last words, that landlady wrote,
were, *I have a daughter.*

Responsible

–for my daughter

We spay our dogs because
it's the responsible thing to do—

too many in the world with fleas,
ticks, worms, mange, what-have-you,

festering with sores, neglected, underfed—
but still—I can't help thinking

about that other responsibility,
to the nature that wants one thing:

to reproduce itself—what she, my dog,
would do if she found herself with puppies.

Did these come from me? she might ask,
the way she asks me everything,

watching them wiggle, cuddle, put up
their tiny mouths to nurse, letting them,

feeling good, watching with delight
as they grew and became playmates,

little toys and friends, as I watched you.

Valentine

When did I fall in love with you?
Was it when I saw you bundled
nose to bottom with your brothers
or the moment you decided to detach,
explore, and I admired your intellect,
aplomb? Or was it when at last
you discovered—not me, exactly,
but my toes—and waddled over
for a nibble, spaniel mine?
You found I had two feet,
finished one, then started on the other.
Licking my toes became your sacrament,
sandals that led me into the barn
that hot June morning, my salvation.

Ghost

> *–the outline of absence defined*
> –from "Kill the Day" by Donald Hall

When she comes to see me now
on a new leash

with her sad eyes

she walks on soft paws
through my new rooms

with the old chairs
and the memory

of her master
inside.

The ghost she's become
is their absence defined:

his ghost and hers,

the door closed forever
behind.

The Urge to Kiss Animals

Delilah, a horse enjoying the sun,
her long nose looking deliciously
kissable

and those cows, grazing together
in the field as I drive by, wanting
to stop

have them turn to me with their
dear, sweet faces

so I can stroke and kiss

and of course this spaniel with
sad eyes and wagging bump tail

looks like she needs a big buss
right on top of her furry head.

Oh, dear—what's to become of me?
How long before they drag me off,

the crazy old lady who goes around
kissing animals where they live?

*Take her home. Tell her to stay
where she belongs.*

Stay out of other people's fields,
their barns, I tell myself.

The sheep don't want you. Neither
do the goats.

Dogs and horses? Maybe.

The Milking

Almost unbearably intimate
to be grasping the body parts
of a being as mammalian
as myself—allowing me to do
this to her, my fingers pulling
like this, the drops from her
body tinkling into the pail
and then, as I grow stronger,
streaming into it, she turning
her head slightly to face me.
She and I producing this—
Satisfaction—together, not
taboo but approved of and
wholesome. All over the world,
I think, men and women are
doing this to females in their
barns—to the great, surrendering
cows who yield themselves
to callused thumbs and fingers,
who let—no, even *beg* these
dominating creatures to do
this to them and who feel,
when the pail is full, *relieved.*

Relatives

I know we share genes
with all kinds of creatures—
even critters—the nasty, squirmy ones.
But *trees?* 'C'mon, *Science Times,*
can it really be?

No wonder I cried
when my sugar maple died
and our dog blessed the hole
right away

and those pear trees on Main
they dug up and threw out--
I mourned for them, too.
Good grief—why?

But now that I find
the Bristlecone Pine
goes back thousands of years
and can live thousands more

It means that I and even you
may be here, too.
So *hip, hip hooray!*
I guess.
Yes?

The Slowest Step

I dreamt I saw my mother in the room
but first the slowest step I ever heard—

tap, tap, tap—until

the door creaked open; there she stood,
a dachshund running fast to greet

as if he knew her. "Is that your dog?"
I asked.

"No, *mine*," a voice behind me said,
(the relative I was visiting that day)

and now it was beginning to get dark,
yet here she was, first time since '93

One hundred thirteen years and there she stood,
out of breath but whole—somehow alive

while we were drinking tea and waiting
for my grandfather, due to arrive soon, too.

The slowest step had brought her here to us.

"I couldn't understand the conductor," she said,
"When he was telling me about the field."

Apparently, she'd crossed a field to get here.

"Mommy!" I cried. "Would you like a cup of tea?"

Still slow of step, she hobbled to the couch,
sat down beside us. I got up; she stayed.

If Grandpa came at last, I never knew.

Split-Screen

While I take pleasure in my right-size plate
and coffee mug of shiny indigo
a twelve-year-old with a toy gun is shot

and another gets juvie for writing on a wall.
What she wrote was *"Hi!"*; I wrote worse
on a white wall at home in our kitchen

at thirteen, age of reason if not sense.
At five, I waved a silver pistol while
playing cops and robbers in the street

with my holster and spurs. Forgive me
if cowboys and cops got mixed up.
I hadn't seen too many movies then

and the "cop on the corner" was my friend.

Gratitude

It was her pleasure
to tell me of my flaws.
Had she not been my mother
I might not have known
my skin was sallow
so not to wear
gray or mustard yellow
or any shade, she said,
of green.
Without her, would I
have ever noticed
my crooked pinky,
the bump on my nose
still there years after
the horse threw me—
and later still
the dust on window-sills
in what she called
my "career-girl" flat?
Surely not.

Her Wit and Wisdom After My Divorce

> *A woman needs a man like a fish*
> *needs a bicycle –Irina Dunn*

"You have so much
to offer a man,"
my mother would say
back when friends and I
were talking about fish and bicycles.

"Offer?" I would ask.
Offer?" thinking
collection plate,
long-handled basket
up and down the aisles,
clasp on my pocketbook
empty purse.

Eve, After Banishment

My body is still warm
but soon it may not be.
I know that. I feel
as if I know too much
and not enough.
He said I will have pain
in childbirth. What is
this *childbirth*? What
will make it happen?
And you, dear Adam—
brother and husband
you must *till*.
What is that?
Strange words fill me,
dance in my head.
You will make *bread*.
What is bread?
I have tasted fruit,
the flesh and juice of it—
and so have you
but now
what you bring
is all that I shall eat.
Already something gnaws
that feels like hunger.

II

New York in the 70's

What blew in from the window that summer
felt good but was only recycled—
car horns suspended like carrot shreds
in gelatin. A dog lay dead on the highway

over our heads, and a roach strutted
like a majorette down Lexington.
Gratings trembled and roared, bars
over windows opened to let out passengers
wrapped in newspapers down to their ankles.

Everybody looked like that. Averted faces,
eyes like volcanic ash. One night I
stumbled, felt the pain coming
up from the sidewalk, but had to

let it happen, let the body sprawl
like it was meant to. Everything
that summer took
longer than it had to.

Bully Pulpit, 2001

The President is speaking.
He says, "This is the first war
Of the Twenty-first Century,"
as if because there have been
there will always be wars
till the end of time.
He has been watching
the world according to Disney
the world according to Hasbro
and the designers of the new
G.I. Joes and Janes
with their cute little clothes
and tiny rifles.
He has been watching
the Pearl Harbor movie
and the other one with Tom Hanks.
The President is a boomer.
He wants to make
his cannons go *boom.*
He makes his hands
into the church with the steeple.
He opens the doors
and his fingers go flying.
He says, "We will rid the world
of evil." He says, *"Shazam!"*
"Do you know what happens," we say,
wagging our fingers at our children,

"to little boys who don't do their homework,
who play video games instead?"
But it is too late.
It is past his bedtime
and the people who flew
out of his hands
are buried under his blocks.

Accounting

> *And I will require an accounting*
> *for the death of every human.*
> *—Genesis 8:13*

The President wipes his lips with a snowy napkin.
Buxom wife is smiling across the table.
Esteemed Secretaries on his right and left.
Fork to mouth, he thinks of "accountability."
What does it mean exactly? is what he thinks,
after he thinks, This duck is good.
Crispy skin is what I like the best.
And that sauce she served with it, the pretty maid
in her crisp black uniform, a tasty dish. Oh, yes.
A mouthful word, if ever there was one.
What was it that new preacher said this morning?
"I will require a counting," I think it was.
If this is what it means—I have a list.
"It's not as if I don't know how to count."

Elephant

At dinner parties
no one speaks of it
because no one knows,
lifting a fork or spoon,
whether others can see
the massive creature
who stands at the thresh-
old looking in—trunk
curling over the table,
mouth opening wide—
the way the one
at the zoo would always
do for me, shoulder-
hoisted so I could drop
a peanut in, and watch
as it disappeared.

Crotch-grab

The first time I saw
a man grabbing his crotch
was in New Jersey
when I stopped for gas
in a strange town.
Something about me—
glasses? briefcase?
must have ticked him off
because he looked me straight
in the eye as he
clicked off the pump.
Insult? Come-on?
Sudden itch?

The next time was when
my painter got down
from his pick-up in the drive
with two guys behind him
and I started talking about
oil base, latex, acrylics.
He was like, *You* talkin' to *me*
about *paint?* And then he
grabbed it, gave it a heave
so I had to notice. Watch
my step? Or, as with Elvis,
wait breathlessly for him
to—actually—unzip?

I know this look now,
the "about-to-grab-don't
mess-with-me" look.

So last night, watching
a candidate gorilla-strut
on TV, I kept wondering
whether he'd really lose it,
grab that crotch with
the whole world looking,
but mostly I kept thinking
how I'd never let him
put up his ladder
against my house.

The New Man

We were having an argument—
not a strong one but a mild disagreement.
He was quiet as I expressed my opinion
and then said, "It's not attractive—"

as if *that* should put an end to my
opinion-stating—
as if my sole desire should be to make
myself attractive to and for him.

Holy be-Jesus. He was gay and out
and I had thought we could be, if not
lovers at least good friends. But would
any woman friend have said that?

Which was when I realized that, gay or not,
a man is still a man—and this one, certainly
was—and then remembered how, on
every occasion when we were together,

he had said or done something like this.
Like that colleague at work, whose reports
I was assigned to edit. "You don't know your place,"
he said when I found flaws. *My job. My place.*

Abram Returns from Battle without Spoils

Sarai, listen—
be glad I'm here—alive.
So? Empty-handed—so what?
Be glad. Be glad.
Which would you rather have—
me, in one piece—or some chattel?
What? Another cow?
A gold bracelet, earrings, fancy cloth?
Should I have brought back
one of their women, eh?
another wife for me?
Ah! I can tell by your eyes
you wouldn't like that at all.
Come here, Cupcake.
Give your old man a kiss—
and draw my bath.

Politics

The politics of envy
The politics of greed
The politics of revenge
The politics of fear
The politics of I've got mine
The politics of lock 'em up
The politics of ethnicity
The politics of race
The politics of piety
The politics of closed doors
The politics of justice
The politics of hate
The politics of open arms
The politics of turned backs
The politics of one percent
The politics of any percent
The politics of shout it out
The politics of civility
The politics of he's a wimp
The politics of anti-
The politics of pro-
The politics of *yes, we can*
The politics of *I don't care*
The politics of *You should.*

To Market, To Market: An American Ghazal

—we're forced to enter the market
just to live
    —Corey Robin in The New York Times

We're forced to enter the market just to live.
My time is up; the battery is dead.

Or maybe a new battery's not all
I'm forced to enter the market for to live.

If I want to know the time, I'll buy a clock
I'm forced to enter the market for to live.

But if I buy the book I can't buy more
I'm forced to enter the market for to live.

If this is all, what are we living for?
The market will survive, with or without

me as a willing participant—or you,
forced to enter the market just to live.

Impeached

If I get impeached, POTUS says,
the stock market will crash—
and everybody

will be very poor.

What would/will impeachment do,
anyway?

Perhaps the poor
will have to sell their stocks.

Oh, my, says a homeless man;
my portfolio's down

along with my socks!

It's the market, the market
that's done me in.

Defiant Subject

Weird rulers
often promulgate
weird solutions
to the problems
of the day.

Pliny the Elder
for example
said you could
cure a cold
by kissing
the hairy muzzle
of a mouse—

which I have never
cared to try
still hoping, as I
do each day
not to find signs

that field mice
have been nibbling
at the clothes
in my closet
or under the hood
of my car.

So, Your Excellency,
I must demur—
or would have
had I lived
under the reign
of a czar.

On Reading Howard Zinn

American history was always such a bore
before.

European much more fun:
blood, beheadings, gore.

Americans had some, too:
scalps and all that—

But in our schoolbooks
even the blood

was red, white and blue.

Downloadable Gun Clears Some Legal Obstacles

—The New York Times, July 14, 2018

Dear Abby,

What do I do if my teenage son
is at his computer downloading
plans for a gun, and last Christmas
we bought him a 3-D printer?
    —Responsible Mom

Dear Responsible,

Pray. Or raid his room. No,
seriously—have you taught him
right—or Right from Wrong?
If so, no harm done. If not,
him have his gun. Or don't.

As for what I think, may you
both—oh, I don't know.
Maybe you'll get lucky
and stay alive—which you
probably will—or maybe not.

And if you don't, well then
maybe we'll all get lucky
and someone will pop
that kid and you two
in the clink
is what I think.

Stay in touch. If not in this
paper, which is short-staffed,
then online, okay? God bless

you and all your neighbors,
young and old, with, without.
      –Abby

Neuticles

> *–The Secret Price of Pets*
> *(The New York Times, July 5, 2018)*

I thought I had
heard it all
seen it all
done it all—

Now learn I hadn't
But still am
one up on you
if you haven't heard

of Neuticles.

Ah, yes, we must protect
some owners say
the "dignity and self-esteem"
of our neutered male dogs

and so they buy prosthetic
testicles, called *neuticles*.
Of course it helps
male (or female) owners
when their pets sport
danglers—
rhinestoned, perhaps,
or be-ribboned. Why not?

Discovery

Conversation with a woman, he said,
as if he'd never had it,

while I, whose words ran through me
like a sieve,

sat there astonished that I had
so much to give

I'd never withheld, and now
this sudden wealth

had found me, as it were,
by stealth—

quite literally in the night
as pastorally

he counseled, complimented
what I little knew

had been my strongest suit:
not beauty, charm, grace,
or even strength of will
but simply talk—
the give-and-take of dialogue

with a man.

Freckled Hands

When my doctor tells me he's going to retire
he lets me know, in more detail than before,
everything that's wrong with me
and what I must watch out for.
Thirty years or more I've been coming down
and waiting to be called in, like a child
outside the principal's office.
Now I watch his white, freckled hands
open a thick folder with my upside-down name,
uncap a fountain pen, and write.
"Having writ," he moves on
and so must I.
I must pick one of three names
he passes across the desk,
the name of someone with a ballpoint,
an efficient, brusque secretary
and a laptop—
someone whose bald head doesn't
gleam under the overhead light
and who has no freckles
on his long white hands.

Allergy

—A cold is the body's weeping.
A physician, quoted somewhere.

Knowing it had been mended
but forgetting the hairline crack

I set my heart down hard
and broke it back

in two, where it had been
once, and once more

drew a quarantine
around my door

and when I had the tests
for pollen, cold and flu

I learned from the allergist,
"a cold, for you,

is more than just a cold;
it's an allergy, too."
One cry breeds another;
the sniffle multiplies.

The body weeps its cold
allergic to goodbyes.

Remembering Her Life

"There was the man," she said,
who wanted to play me again
like an old record,
read me once more
like a well-loved book."

"I can't say that I blame him
or that I'm offended.
Flattered, rather—
by the wreath of memory,
the laurel of desire."

Solo

I never imagined myself
leading a team to glory—
just wanted to be the one
dancing in a cone of light
or standing, arched
on the edge of the board,
seeing only the blue
of the deeper end,
chlorine rising like perfume,
water parting to let me in
silent to the bottom
then up to where air was,
lifting myself out,
pulling off my cap,
letting dark hair spill
till they handed me
gardenias to hold it back,
their scent like love itself:
that drowning.

In Grief

The flat-faced women in his poems—
did I say *poems*
when what I mean is *paintings*—
things on canvas
or boards.
stretched on easels
hanging on gallery walls
or mine—
those flat-faced women
are hiding something,
but *what?*
and why do I understand?

Dialogue in Green

> *–in memoriam, Will Barnet (1911-2012)*

I bought it with an honorarium—
the girl-woman whose dark hair was like mine,
back toward me on the Turkish rug,
(a *kilim*, I learned later it was called,
and the girl who posed was his daughter).
Her cat looked toward me, hunched along
the border, eyes two slits of light
in black fur, brown paneling behind it.
The girl's hair long, strands like black
cats' tails over the shoulders of her dull
green robe, one hand on a gray diamond
of the rug's design, on the same plane
as the cat's eyes, the same white, as if
the energy in her hand lighted the eyes, and
the cat knew how they held each other in silence.
The secret they shared on the rug was mine,
burnt orange on green, dark and lighter red,
gray, black, white – all mine when I left the gallery,
its muted loveliness rolled under my arm.
Linen-matted, framed in wood I stained walnut,
it moved with me five times.

Somewhere in those years I met him at River Gallery,
with his blonde wife. An exhibit of his serigraphs.
He looked like anyone, a man in his late sixties,
seventies, perhaps, a lawyer, an accountant—while

around us on the walls dark-haired women stared at cats,
linoleum, coffee cups, out to sea, and behind him
a child looked gravely from a frame, one hand
over a top, the other resting lightly on a ball.
The dark verticals of trees echoed the gowns
of women gliding among them, standing—
the same woman, fragmented, now this way, now that,
her long hair still down, or in a twist at the nape,
like part of a waiting animal, stillness at her center.

All his women were waiting—his blonde wife,
the beaming gallery owner, me in a tweed jacket
(it was Saturday, fall). He was bald, I remember,
pleasant, businesslike, with a good but not
aggressive sense of his market worth. I told him
I had an artist's impression of *Dialogue in Green*.

"Good. They're hard to find now," he said.

I felt congratulated, almost smug, but lacking
something I must have looked for in that meeting—

and looked for anew when another green
entered our dialogue. Home from vacation after
a wet July and wetter August, I found the creeping
green of mildew under my picture's glass, green
paneling, the kilim, even the girl's dark hair.

Dollars helped restore it. Dollars I barely had.
But the girl—the dark-haired girl
I must have wanted to be that day—
is back over my couch
and still stares silently at the cat.

Aubade for the Almost-Old

Gas station worker accused of credit fraud!
Woman has identity stolen!
Storm heads up East Coast!

Breakfast punctuated with alarms
I read aloud with exclamation points.
My husband chews his bite-size Shredded Wheat.
I pour myself more coffee, then get ready
to defend myself and us against the day.

What shall we do first?
make love carefully?
Prepare our records for the IRS?
Put on hip boots to wade around our cellar?
Scrub our fruit with anti-bacterials?

Arrange a couple of balance transfers?
Make an appointment for a root canal?
See the estate planner who specializes
in conserving non-existent assets?
Look over long-term care brochures?

Install the budget-management software?
Or go to the bookstore and ring up
another batch we won't have time to read?

Old in a Time of Pandemic

Waking, she wonders
if this day will be her last
or another of the same old
obscuring all but thoughts
of time past and reconsidered
before it all became
just one damn thing after another.
Does she dare to take a breath
or a break?
Grab a mint
or the handle
of her cane?
Tuck a short
umbrella in her purse
in case of rain?
On second thought
or third
or even more—
how is this
any different
from before?

Lockdown Sonnet

I don't want to think
about how a sonnet turns
and whether what follows the *volte*
is truly what it earns.
My only hope is that
It will make sense to you,
Dear Reader, on whose good will
I so depend—that you
will get my drift—my recompense
for trying to make sense
of what essentially
has none, or perhaps is not
even dignifiable
as non-sense.

Fully Engaged

In lifelong self-
analysis
I wanted the world
to help me do it
but held a little back.

If you didn't hear
or read it
I didn't really know
or even care.

Was that self-aware
self-centered
selfish—or what?

Gen-X has a word:
over-share
as if it's a fault
(perhaps a crevasse).

My Pleasure

The wine runs over the garage floor
and people are walking in the wine
and people are walking into the building
 their toes wet with wine.
The wine bottle is lying on its side
and its broken neck threatens tires
and I try to give him a dollar.

I wait with my dollar and my shopping bag
but he is too busy parking cars
and I wait watching my spilled wine spread
watching how it runs
and when he returns he won't take it.

Won't take my dollar   my pleasure, he says.
My pleasure in eighty-five degrees.
My pleasure on Eighty-fifth Street.
My pleasure in the office with the TV on
and the door open.

It will cut their tires I say.
Did you cut your hand he says.
No I say with the dollar please.
My pleasure he says from behind another wheel.
My pleasure.

A Life

I learned to talk
I learned to walk
I learned to play

I went to school
I learned to read
I learned to write

I rode a bike
I flew a kite
I learned to skate

I learned to swim
I learned to dance
I sang some songs

I rode a horse
I rode a train
I hailed a cab

I walked a dog
I fed a cat
I milked a cow

I wrote some poems
I learned to knit
I planted seeds

I mowed some grass
I learned to love
and not to hate

I never did
learn how to dive
but felt the glory

of being alive.
I went to church
and knelt to pray

To my surprise
God answered me
"Oy vey," said They –

"you wanted *more?*"

Laughing Kookaburras
(Australian Birds)

Are they sexy
>do they still mate?

If so, we can hope

>or imagine

a world filled
with laughing kookaburras

and children

calling their names.

About the Author

Irene Willis has published five collections of poetry: *They Tell Me You Danced* (University Press of Florida, 1995); *At the Fortune Café* (recipient of the 2005 Violet Reed Haas Award and a National Book Award nominee; *Those Flames* (Bay Oak Publishers, Ltd., 2009); *Reminder* (Word Poetry, 2014); and *Rehearsal* (IPBooks, 2018). She has also edited two anthologies, both published by IPBooks): *Climate of Opinion: Sigmund Freud in Poetry* (IPBooks, 2017) and *What*

They Bring: The Poetry of Migration and Immigration, co-edited with Jim Haba. (IPBooks, 2020). Her poems have also appeared in many journals and anthologies, both print and online. Awards for her poetry include a Distinguished Artist Fellowship from the New Jersey State Council on the Arts, a residency fellowship from the Millay Colony for the Arts, and grants from the Massachusetts Cultural Council and the Berkshire/Taconic Foundation.

She attended St. Lawrence University, holds a B.S. in Education from SUNY Fredonia, a Ph.D. in Educational Leadership from New York University and MFA in Poetry from New England College.

Having taught for many years in high schools, colleges and graduate schools, most recently at Westfield State University and American International College, she is now retired and living in the Berkshires in Western Massachusetts, where she works from home as a free-lance writer and editor.

An emeritus member of the Authors' Guild, she is also an Educator Associate of the International Psychoanalytic Association and Poetry Editor of the online publication, International Psychoanalysis (*www.internationalpsychoanalysis.net*), where she has a monthly column called *Poetry Monday.*

Acknowledgments

The Bark: "Valentine"

Ekphrastic Review: "Dialogue in Green"

Except for Love: New England Poets Inspired by Donald Hall: "Ghost," and "The Milking"

Mudfish: "I Was the Girl Who Always Spoke" and "The Letters in My Dream"

Paterson Literary Review: "Fresh Start"

U.S.1 Worksheets: "House" and "My Story and Yours"

As always, I would like to acknowledge Olivia VanSant, P.A. *extraordinaire;* my wonderful computer consultant, Ernie Lowell, and my beloved Springer Spaniel, Abigail, who is somehow always with us, in spirit or as herself, when we work on anything connected with poems.

I am forever grateful for the supportive fellowship of Lisken Van Pelt Dus, Cynthia Gardner, Hilary Russell, Phil Timpane, our U.K. member, Chris Fogg, my morning poetry buddy, David Giannini, and my friend and neighbor, Bud Aronson, who helps me so much at readings.

Gratitude also to Tamar and Larry Schwartz at IPBooks, for always being there and for doing whatever needs to be done, whenever.

CPSIA information can be obtained
at www.ICGtesting.com
Printed in the USA
FSHW021449110221
78470FS